The Dyer and Colour Maker's Companion

Henry Carey Baird

THE

DYER AND COLOUR MAKER'S

COMPANION:

CONTAINING UPWARDS OF

TWO HUNDRED RECEIPTS FOR MAKING COLOURS

ON THE MOST APPROVED PRINCIPLES,

FOR

ALL THE VARIOUS STYLES AND FABRICS NOW IN EXISTENCE.

TOGETHER WITH

THE SCOURING PROCESS,

AND PLAIN DIRECTIONS FOR PREPARING, WASHING-OFF,

AND FINISHING THE GOODS.

NEW EDITION.

PHILADELPHIA:

HENRY CAREY BAIRD,

No. 406 WALNUT ST.

1860.

COLLINS, PRINTER.

CONTENTS.

SECTION I.—MORDANTS FOR MADDER DYING.

SECTION II.—STEAM COLOURS FOR LINEN & COTTON.

CONTENTS.

SECTION III.—FAST COLOURS FOR RAISING IN LIME OR SODA LIQUOR.

SECTION IV.—CHEMICAL COLOURS.

CONTENTS.

SECTION V.—RESISTING BLUE VAT COLOURS.

SECTION VI.—TURKEY RED DYEING.

How to Prepare Cloth for Dyeing.

SECTION VII.—ORANGE DYEING.

SECTION VIII.—COLOURS FOR YELLOW GROUNDS.

SECTION IX.—SILK DYEING.

SECTION X.—MOUSSELINE D'LAINE PRINTING.

CONTENTS.

SECTION XI.—STANDARDS FOR VARIOUS SHADES.

SECTION XII.—MISCELLANEOUS RECEIPTS.

FRENCH ORANGES.—MORDANTS.

THE

DYER AND COLOUR MAKER'S COMPANION.

SECTION I.

MORDANTS FOR MADDER DYING.

No. 1.

TO MAKE LIGHT PURPLE FOR ONE COLOUR ON JACONETS.

58 Measures of Water.
  2   Do.   Acetic Acid, 8° Twaddell.
  1   Do.   Iron Liquor, 32°   do.
    Thicken with Flour or Gum, as No. 7.

Note.—Purple Mordants are made from common Iron Liquor, and Pyroligneous or Acetic Acid: the latter is considered best for light shades.

(9)

No. 2.

DARK PURPLE COLOUR.

1 Measure Iron Liquor, 32° Twaddell.
1   Do.   Acetic Acid, 8°   do.
Reduce with water to 4°   do.
Thicken with Flour.

No. 3.

LIGHT PURPLE FOR TWO COLOURS.

22 Measures Water.
 2   Do.   Acetic Acid, 8° Twaddell.
 1   Do.   Iron Liquor, 32°   do.
Thicken with Flour or Gum, as No. 7.

No. 4.

LIGHT CHOCOLATE COLOUR.

3 Gallons Red Liquor, 8° Twaddell.
1   Do. Iron do   8°   do.
3 ℔s. British Gum,   ⎱
6 ℔s. American Flour, ⎰ to thicken.
1 Pint Logwood Liquor, 8° Twaddell.
Boil Thirty Minutes.

No. 5.

DARK CHOCOLATE COLOUR.

3 Gallons Iron Liquor, 8° Twaddell.
1 Do. Red do. 8° do.
3 lbs. British Gum, ⎫
6 lbs. American Flour, ⎬ to thicken.
1 Pint Logwood Liquor, 8° Twaddell.
Boil Thirty Minutes.

No. 6.

TO MAKE RED LIQUOR.

12 Gallons Water, 170° Fahrenheit.
36 lbs. Alum.
21 lbs. White Sugar of Lead,—added gradually.
To stand one hour,—then add
1½ lbs. Spanish Whitening.
Mix well together—use the pure Liquor at
16° Twaddell.

No. 7.

LIGHT RED COLOUR.

6 Measures Water.
1   Do.   Red Liquor, 16° Twaddell.
    Thicken with Flour or British Gum.
       When Gum is used, take
6 Gallons Water.
36 ℔s. Gum,—Boil well.—Ready for use in 3
days.—Darken with Peachwood Liquor.

No. 8.

DARK RED COLOUR.

3 Gallons Red Liquor, 12° Twaddell.
6 ℔s. American Flour,—to thicken.
      Boil well.
1 Pint Peachwood Liquor 8° Twad. to darken.

No. 9.

BLACK COLOUR.

1 Gallon Iron Liquor, 5° Twaddell.
1 Quart Acetic Acid, 8°   do.
1½ lbs. Flour,
  ½ lb. British Gum, } to thicken,
  ½ Pint Logwood Liquor, 8° Twad.—to darken.

No. 10.

BROWN COLOUR.

1 Gallon Acetic Acid, 8° Twaddell.
2 Quarts Water.
10 lbs. Catechu.
2½ lbs. Salammoniac.
  Dissolve—let stand 12 hours—then add
2 Gallons Gum Substitute.
1½ Pints Red Liquor, 16° Twaddell.
1½ Do. Nitrate of Copper, 70° do.

No. 11.

E GUM SUBSTITUTE LIQUOR.

6 lbs. Substitute, $\Big\}$ Boil One Hour.
1 Gallon Water,

No. 12.

AMBER OR GOLD COLOUR.

1 Gallon Bark Liquor, 16° Twaddell.
2 lbs. Starch.
Boil 30 Minutes,—cool to 130° Fah.—then add
2 lbs. Sulphate of Zinc,—dissolve.

SECTION II.

STEAM COLOURS FOR LINEN & COTTON.

No. 13.

TO PREPARE CLOTH PREVIOUS TO PRINTING,

Take 18 Measures Caustic Potash Lye, 16° Twad.

    1   Do.   Oxymuriate of Tin, 120° do.

Mix well together, and reduce with Water to 12° Twaddell.

Note.—Put the cloth through the Liquor, 10 Pieces on the Beam; let stand Two Hours; then put through Vitriol Sour at 3° Twaddell,—wash for 10 Minutes, and dry.

No. 14.

CAUSTIC POTASH LYE.

20 Gallons Water, 212° Fahrenheit.
40 ℔s. American Potash,—dissolve, then add
20 ℔s. Irish Lime.

No. 15.

LIGHT CHOCOLATE COLOUR.

9 Quarts Sapanwood Liquor, 8° Twaddell.
9   Do. Water.
6   Do. Logwood Liquor, 12°   do.
3   Do. Red Liquor, 16°   do.
12 Oz. Salammoniac.
12 Oz. Sulphate of Copper.
12 Oz. Alum.
3½ ℔s. British Gum.
13½ ℔s. Flour.
       Boil Thirty Minutes.

No. 16.

RED CHOCOLATE COLOUR.

3 Gallons Sapanwood Liquor, 9° Twaddell.
3 Quarts Nitrate of Alumina.
1½ Gallons Logwood Liquor,   9°   do.
6 Oz. Yellow Prussiate of Potash.
6 Oz. Red   do.   do.
9 lbs. Starch,—to thicken.
            Boil Thirty Minutes.

No. 17.

RED COLOUR.

6 Quarts Sapanwood Liquor, 9° Twaddell.
1 Do. Nitrate of Alumina.
1 Do. Persian Berry Liquor, 12° do.
4 lbs. Starch.
2 Oz. Chloride of Potash.
            Boil Thirty Minutes.

No. 18.

NITRATE OF ALUMINA FOR CHOCOLATE.

1 Gallon Water, 212° Fahrenheit.
3 ℔s. Nitrate of Lead.
3 ℔s. Alum.

Dissolve, and add

½ ℔. Soda.—Use Pure Liquor only.

No. 19.

NITRATE OF ALUMINA FOR RED.

1 Gallon Water, 212° Fahrenheit.
4 ℔s. Nitrate of Lead.
4 ℔s. Alum.

Dissolve, as No. 18.

No. 20.

PINK COLOUR.

1 Gallon Pink Standard.
2   Do. Senegal Gum Liquor.

No. 21.

COCHINEAL PINK STANDARD.

1 Gallon Cochineal Liquor, 6° Twaddell, 170°
    Fahrenheit.
6 Oz. Alum.
3 Oz. Tartrate of Potash.
½ Oz. Oxalic Acid.
                    Dissolve.

No. 22.

SCARLET COLOUR.

1 Gallon Cochineal Liquor, 6° Twaddell.
2 lbs. Starch.
Boil Thirty Minutes,—Cool to 150° Fahrenheit,
                    then add
3 Oz. Muriate of Tin Crystals.
            Cool to 110° Fah.—add
5 Oz. Superoxalate of Potash, and
1 Pint Bark Liquor, 12° Twaddell.

No. 23.

LAVENDER OR PALE PURPLE STANDARD.

10 Gallons Red Liquor, 16° Twad., 190° Fah.
30 lbs. Ground Logwood.
10 Oz. Super-oxalate of Potash.
10 Oz. Oxalic Acid.
Mix together,—stand Twenty-four Hours.—Use the Liquor only.   Thicken with Senegal Gum.

No. 24.

DARK ROYAL PURPLE COLOUR.

1 Gallon Logwood Liquor, 6° Twaddell.
4 lbs. Senegal Gum, at 180° Fahrenheit.
8 Oz. Red Prussiate of Potash.
12 Oz. Alum.
1 Oz. Oxalic Acid.
2 Oz. Superoxalate of Potash.
Dissolve.

No. 25.

BROWN COLOUR.

3 Quarts Persian Berry Liquor, 12° Twaddell.
3　Do.　Bark Liquor,　　　12°　do.
2　Do.　Sapan Extract.
3　Do.　Pale Purple Standard.
2　Do.　Logwood Liquor, 12° Twaddell.
12 ℔s. Substitute.
12 Oz. Alum.
8 Oz. Salammoniac.
8 Oz. Sulphate of Copper.
　　Boil Thirty Minutes.—When cold, add
1 Noggin Nitrate of Copper, 8° Twaddell.

No. 26.

DARK ROYAL PURPLE.

2 Gallons Water. ⎫
4 ℔s. Starch.　　⎬ Boil 30 Minutes, then add
　　　　　　　　⎭
6 ℔s. Tartaric Acid.—Dissolve, and add
1 Gallon Prussiate of Tin.—Mix well, and add
6 ℔s. Yellow Prussiate of Potash, and
3 Oz. Oxalic Acid.

No. 27.

PRUSSIATE OF TIN.

8 Gallons Water, 180° Fahrenheit.
8 ℔s. Prussiate of Potash.
       Dissolve,—then take
5 Gallons Water.
4 Quarts Muriate of Tin, 120° Fahrenheit.
       Mix together,—and add
12 Gallons Water.
       Filter to the consistency of a Paste.

No. 28.

BLACK COLOUR.

3	Gallons Logwood Liquor,	12°	Twaddell.	
1	Do. Red Liquor,	16°	do.	
1	Do. Iron Liquor,	30°	do.	
1	Do. Acetic Acid,	8°	do.	

7½ ℔s. Flour.
3 ℔s. British Gum.
       Boil Thirty Minutes.

No. 29.

YELLOW COLOUR.

2 Gallons Berry Liquor, 6° Twaddell.
3 lbs. Starch.

Boil, and add

4 Oz. Muriate of Tin Crystals.

Cool to 110° Fahrenheit, and add

1 Oz. Oxalic Acid.

No. 30.

DARK GREEN.

3   Quarts Bark Liquor, 12° Twaddell.
3   Do.   Persian Berry Liquor, 6° do.
6   lbs. Substitute.
1½ lbs. Alum.

Boil Thirty Minutes, and add

6   Oz. Double Muriate of Tin, 120° Twaddell.
1   Pint Acetic Acid,   8°   do.
3   lbs. Prussiate of Potash.
1   Pint Prussiate of Tin.

Mix well.

No. 31.

PALE GREEN STANDARD.

1 Gallon Water, 170° Fahrenheit.
2 lbs. 10 oz. Prussiate of Potash.
Dissolve,—then take
2 Gallons Gum, add to which
12 Oz. Double Muriate of Tin, 120° Twaddell.
1 Gill Acetic Acid, 8° do.
Mix all together,—then take
2 Gallons Persian Berry Liquor, 12° Twad.
1½ lbs. Alum.
Boil, and mix with preceding ingredients.

No. 32.

AMBER OR GOLD.

7 Quarts Persian Berry Liquor, 6° Twaddell.
1 Do. Cochineal, 4° do.
3 lbs. Starch.
Boil, and add
6 Oz. Muriate of Tin Crystals.
Cool to 110° Fahrenheit, and add
1 Oz. Oxalic Acid.

No. 33.

OLIVE STANDARD COLOUR.

6 Quarts Berry Liquor, 12° Twaddell.
12 Oz. Alum.

Boil, and add

1 Quart Dark Purple.
1 Do. Logwood Liquor, 8° Twaddell.

Mix together.

No. 34.

DARK PURPLE FOR OLIVE.

7 Quarts of Pale Purple Standard.
1 Gallon Logwood Liquor, 12° Twaddell.
1 Noggin Nitrate of Copper, 120° do.

No. 35.

OLIVE COLOUR.

1 Measure Olive Standard.
8 Do. Gum.

No. 36.

DRAB STANDARD.

1　Gallon Persian Berry Liquor, 12° Twad.
7　lbs. Substitute.
　　Boil,—cool to 130° Fahrenheit, —add
1½ lbs. Alum.
1　lb. Sulphate of Iron.
1　Quart Fresh Logwood Liquor, 2° Twaddell.
1　Do. Cochineal Liquor.　　3°　　do.

No. 37.

DARK DAHLIA.

6　Quarts Pink Standard.
1　　Do.　Pale Purple Standard.
5　lbs. Substitute.
　　　Boil Thirty Minutes.

No. 38.

LIGHT DAHLIA.

6 Quarts Pink Standard.
2   Do.   Light Purple Standard.
6   Do.   Gum Water.

No. 39.

STONE STANDARD.

2 Quarts Pale Purple Standard.
1   Do.   Common Blue.
2   Do.   Pink Standard.
              Mix well.

No. 40.

COMMON BLUE STANDARD.

2 Gallons Water.
4 lbs. Prussiate of Potash.
12 Oz. Alum.
24 Oz. Vitriol.—Dissolve.

No. 41.

COMMON BLUE COLOUR.

2 Quarts Gum Water.
1   Do. Blue Standard.
1 Glass Extract of Indigo.

No. 42.

FAWN STANDARD.

3 Quarts No. 3 Yellow.
1 Pint Pink Standard.
1 Gill Pale Purple Standard.

No. 43.

No. 3 YELLOW.

1 Gallon Berry Liquor, 3° Twaddell.
3 ℔s. Substitute.
6 Oz. Alum.
Boil Thirty Minutes.

No. 44.

SLATE STANDARD.

2 Quarts Pale Purple Standard.
3 Pints Common Blue.

No. 45.

SLATE COLOUR.

1 Quart Standard.
3 Do. Gum Water.

No. 46.

BLUE COLOUR FOR BLACK GROUND.

2 Gallons Water.
2¼ ℔s. Prussiate of Potash.
18 Oz. Alum.
6 Oz. Tartaric Acid.
1 Gallon Gum Water.
3 Gills Double Muriate of Tin, 120° Twad.
Mix. well.

No. 47.

LAVENDER COLOUR.

6 Quarts Pale Purple Standard.
1   Do.   Common Blue Colour.
3   Do.   Gum Water.

No. 48.

CINNAMON COLOUR.

8 Quarts Sapanwood Liquor, 6° Twaddell.
1   Do.   Alumina for Red.
2   Do.   Brown Colour.
12   Do.   Gum Water.

No. 49.

DISCHARGE WHITE FOR ROYAL BLUE.

2 Gallons Caustic Potash Lye, 40° Twaddell.
2 lbs. British Gum.
          Boil Thirty Minutes.

SECTION III.

FAST COLOURS FOR RAISING IN LIME OR SODA LIQUOR.

No. 50.

FAST BLUE STANDARD.

6 Quarts Caustic Potash Lye, 30° Twaddell.
3   Do.   4-℔. Indigo.
4 ℔s. Granulated Tin.
Boil Six Hours: keep up to Six Quarts with Water.—To stand Twelve Hours.

No. 51.

BLUE COLOUR.

3 Quarts Standard.
1   Do.   Double Muriate of Tin, 120° Twad.
      Mix very well, and add
6 Quarts Gum Water.

Note.—This Colour can only be used when Fresh.

No. 52.

GREEN.

3 Quarts Fast Blue.
1   Do. Nitrate of Lead Liquor.
Mix well.

No. 53.

R   NITRATE OF LEAD LIQUOR.

4 lbs. Nitrate of Lead.
1 Gallon Water.
2 lbs. Substitute.
Dissolve.

No. 54.

BUFF STANDARD.

4   Gallons Water.
20   lbs. Sulphate of Iron.
5   lbs. Brown Sugar of Lead.
2½ lbs. White   do.   do.
Dissolve, and add
1   Gallon Water.——Use the Pure Liquor only.

No. 55.

FAST BUFF COLOUR.

1 Gallon Standard.
3   Do. Gum Water

          Mix together.

No. 56.

FAST DRAB STANDARD.

8 Gallons Water.
32 ℔s. Brown Chrome.

Put into a Copper vessel, and carefully observe its depth; then empty it into a Wooden vessel, and add

8 Gallons Water.
5 Quarts Vitriol.

———

Note.—Stir it till Effervescence ceases; return it again into the Copper vessel, and Boil to its original depth.

No. 57.

FAST DRAB COLOUR.

1 Quart Standard.
2 Do. Gum Water.
1 Pint Buff Standard.
1 Quart Water.

No. 58.

FAST BLACK COLOUR.

Ingredients as in No. 28.

No. 59.

CHINA BLUE STANDARD.

1 Gallon 4-lb. Indigo.
2 Quarts Muriate of Iron, 80° Twaddell.
Mix well.

No. 60.

CHINA BLUE COLOUR.

3 Quarts Gum Water.
1 Do. Standard.

No. 61.

TO RAISE CHINA BLUE.

COPPERAS VAT, { 200 Gallons of Water, add
{ 300 ℔s. Sulphate of Iron.
Dissolve to 8° Twaddell.

LIME VAT, { 200 Gallons Water, add
{ 6 Do. Fine Powdered Irish Lime.
Dissolve.

RAISING.—Put 6 32-yard Pieces Cloth on a Beam, and

1st, Run 4 times through Lime Vat.
2d, " 3 "   " Copperas "
3d, " 6 "   " Lime   "
4th, " 3 "   " Copperas "

(*Over.*)

No. 61—Continued.

5th, Run 6 times through Lime Vat.
6th, " 3 " " Copperas "
7th, " 3 " " Lime "
8th, " 2 " " Copperas "

Strip off Beam in Single Pieces, and wash well in pure Water,—run five minutes through Vitriol Sour, 4° Twaddell,—wash fifteen minutes in Wheels,—put into a Clearing Copper, till it reaches 160° Fahrenheit,—then dissolve 3 lbs. White Soap, rinse thirty minutes, wash and finish.

No. 62.

FAST BROWN.

1 Quart Acetic Acid, 8° Twaddell.
2 Do. Water.
3 Do. Catechu.
12 Oz. Salammonia.
1 Quart Gum Water.
1 Pint Nitrate of Copper.

No. 63.

TO RAISE FAST BLUE.

20 Gallons Water.
20 lbs. Soda.
Dissolve.—Rinse Cloth twenty minutes, then wash fifteen minutes in Wheels.

No. 64.

TO RAISE FAST GREEN.

20 Gallons Water.
20 lbs. Soda.
Rinse twenty minutes,—take out and rinse in Chrome Liquor twenty minutes at $1\frac{1}{2}°$ Twaddell,—wash and finish.

Note.—Brown, Buff, and Drab, raised same as No. 63.

SECTION IV.

CHEMICAL COLOURS.

No. 65.

DAHLIA SHADES. A. STANDARD.

3 Quarts Logwood Liquor, 12° Twaddell.

2   Do. Hemetine Liquor.

5 ℔s. Barbary Gum.

    Bring to 110° Fahrenheit, and add

1 Pint Oxymuriate of Tin, 120° Twaddell.

1 Noggin Acetate of Copper.

1   Do. Nitrate of Iron, 80° Twaddell.

No. 66.

B. STANDARD.

3 Quarts Logwood Liquor, 12° Twaddell.

1   Do. Hemetine.

4 Oz. Salammonia.

2 Quarts Barbary Gum Water.

1 Pint Oxymuriate of Tin, 120° Twaddell.

1 Noggin Nitrate of Copper, 80°   do

No. 67.

ACETATE OF COPPER.

4 lbs. Sulphate of Copper.
3 lbs. White Sugar of Lead.
1 Gallon Water.
    Dissolve, and use Pure Liquor only.

No. 68.

PINK STANDARD.

2 Quarts Sapanwood Liquor, 14° Twaddell.
4 Oz. Salammonia.
2 Quarts Barbary Gum Water.
1 Pint Oxymuriate of Tin, 120° Twaddell.

No. 69.

DARK DAHLIA.

6 Pints A. Standard.
2 Do. Pink Standard.
1 Do. Persian Berry Liquor, 12° Twaddell.
    Mix well.

LIGHT DAHLIA.

No. 70.

2 Pints B. Standard.
1 Do. Pink Standard.
1 Quart Barley Gum Water.

No. 71.

DARK PURPLE.

1 Gallon Logwood Liquor, 8° Twaddell.
$1\frac{1}{2}$ ℔s. Starch.
Boil well,—cool to 110° Fahrenheit, and add
1 Pint Oxymuriate of Tin, 120° Twaddell.
1 Gill Nitrate of Iron,   80°   do.
1 Noggin Oil.

No. 72.

LILAC.

1 Gallon Logwood Liquor, 2° Twaddell.
$1\frac{1}{2}$ ℔s. Starch.
Boil well,—cool to 110° Fahrenheit, and add
3 Noggins Oxymuriate of Tin.
$\frac{1}{4}$ Glass Nitrate of Iron, 80° Twaddell.

No. 73.

PINK.

1 Gallon Sapanwood Liquor, 8° Twaddell.
1½ lbs. Starch.
   Boil,—cool to 110° Fahrenheit, and add
3 Noggins Oxymuriate of Tin, 120° Twad.
1   Do.   Acetate of Copper.

No. 74.

PRUSSIAN BLUE.

4 lbs. Prussiate of Potash.
1 Gallon Water.
            Dissolve,—then take
8 lbs. Sulphate of Iron.
1 Gallon Water.
   Dissolve,—mix both together, and add
1 Quart Nitric Acid.
Wash three times, and filter for the pulp.

No. 75.

BLUE.

1 Gallon Water.
1½ lbs. Starch.
  Boil,—cool to 110° Fahrenheit, and add
1 Quart Prussian Blue.
3 Noggins Oxymuriate of Tin.

No. 76.

CHOCOLATE.

3 Quarts Sapanwood Liquor, 8° Twaddell.
2 Do. Logwood do. 8° do.
1 Do. Bark do. 8° do.
2 lbs. Starch.
  Boil,—cool to 110° Fahrenheit, and add
1 Pint Oxymuriate of Tin, 120° Twaddell.
1 Gill Nitrate of Iron, 80° do.
1 Pint Oil.

No. 77.

GREEN.

2 Quarts Blue.
1   Do.   Yellow.   } Mix well.

No. 78.

YELLOW.

1   Gallon Bark Liquor, 12° Twaddell.
1½ lbs. Starch.
  Boil,—cool to 110° Fahrenheit, and add
1   Pint Oxymuriate of Tin, 120° Twaddell.

No. 79.

ORANGE.

3 Quarts Yellow.
1   Do.   Pink.   } Mix.

No. 80.

BROWN.

2 Quarts Chocolate.
1 Do. Yellow. } Mix.
1 Pint Dark Purple.

No. 81.

SLATE.

1 Quart Blue.
1 Do. Dark Purple, } Mix.
4 Do. Gum Water.

No. 82.

DRAB.

2 Quarts Slate.
1 Do. Yellow. } Mix.
1 Gill Pink.

Note.—The Colours in this Section must remain Three Days in a cool place before washing off.

SECTION V.

RESISTING BLUE-VAT COLOURS.

No. 83.

ORANGE PASTE.

3 Gallons Water.
48 lbs. Brown Sugar of Lead.
18 lbs. Vitriol.
Wash three times in pure water, and filter to 3
Gallons,—thicken with—
30 lbs. Pipe Clay.—Take
3 Gallons Gum Water.
12 lbs. Nitrate of Lead.
16 lbs. Sulphate of Copper.
Dissolve,—and mix together.

No. 84.

INNOCENT PASTE OR WHITE.

2   Quarts Water.
8   ℔s. Sulphate of Copper.
1   ℔. Sacrum.
Dissolve,—allow it to remain till Effervescence
            ceases, and thicken with
2½ ℔s. Pipe Clay.
8   Oz. Soft Soap.
2   Quarts Gum Water.

No. 85.

RESIST RED.

5   Gallons Red Liquor, 16° Twaddell.
2½ ℔s. Verdigris,—thicken 3-4ths with
15 ℔s. Pipe Clay, and add to remainder
7   ℔s. Soft Soap Dissolved.
5   Gallons Red Liquor,—thicken with
20 ℔s. Senegal Gum, and
            Mix all together.

No. 86.

DARK RESIST CHOCOLATE.

2 Quarts Resist Red.
1   Do. Iron Liquor, 80° Twaddell. } Mix.

No. 87.

RESIST PALE RED.

$5\frac{1}{2}$ Quarts Innocent Paste.
1   Do. Red Liquor, 16° Twaddell. } Mix.

No. 88.

BLUE PASTE.

1 Gallon Water.
2 lbs. Sulphate of Copper.
4 Oz. Brown Sugar of Lead.
$2\frac{1}{2}$ lbs. Flour.
$1\frac{1}{4}$ lbs. British Gum.
Boil well,—cool to 110° Fahrenheit, and add
1 Gill Nitrate of Copper, 80° Twaddell.

No. 89.

BLUE VAT SETTING.

400 Gallons Water.
 40 lbs. Spanish Indigo.
 70 lbs. Sulphate of Iron.
100 lbs. Irish Lime.
 Dissolve,—to remain Three Days before use.

No. 90.

LIME VATTING.

400 Gallons Water.
200 lbs. Irish Lime.

SECTION VI.

TURKEY RED DYEING.

TO PREPARE CLOTH FOR DYEING.

Take 18 Quarts Gallapola Oil, and mix in 32 Gallons Water, at 160° Fahrenheit.

Take 2 Gallons Water and 4 lbs. Pearl Ashes,—dissolve and mix with the Oil and Water; then—

1st. Run Twice and Dry.

2d. Do. do.

3d. Run Six times, and hang 8 Hours in hot Stove.

Soak in Pearl Ash Liquor, at 1° Twaddell, and 120° Fahrenheit, for 8 Hours; Press and Soak in a fresh Bath, same Heat, Strength, and Time. Repeat Process, and Soak 3 Hours in Pure Water. Wash and Dry.

Note.—If for Plain Red, run in Red Liquor, 12° Twaddell, and Dry. Dye with 2½ lbs. French Madder ⅌ 28-yards ⅞ Cloth.

No. 91.

WHITE DISCHARGE.

1 Gallon Water.
8 lbs. Tartaric Acid.
4 lbs. Pipe Clay.
1 Gallon Barbary Gum Liquor.
Mix.

No. 92.

YELLOW DISCHARGE.

1 Gallon Water.
5 lbs. Tartaric Acid.
6 lbs. Nitrate of Lead.
Dissolve,—thicken with
5 lbs. Pipe Clay, and
1 Gallon Gum Liquor.

No. 93.

GREEN DISCHARGE.

2 Quarts Blue Discharge. } Mix.
1   Do.   Yellow.

No. 94.

BLUE DISCHARGE.

2 Gallons Muriate of Tin, 120° Twaddell.
1   Do.   Prussian Blue.—Then take
1   Do.   Water, and
5 lbs. Tartaric Acid,—Dissolve, and add
2 Quarts of the above, and
2   Do.   Gum Dragon Liquor.

No. 95.

BLACK DISCHARGE.

1 Gallon Logwood Liquor, 4° Twaddell.
2 lbs. Prussiate of Potash.
1 Quart Gum Dragon.
2 lbs. Flour.
2 Quarts Iron Liquor, 30° Twaddell.
   Boil,—Cool to 110° Fahrenheit, and add
1 Gill Nitrate of Iron, 80° Twaddell.

SECTION VII.

ORANGE DYEING.

No. 96.

ORANGE.

60 lbs. Brown Sugar of Lead.
30 lbs. Litharge of Lead.

Dissolve in Boiling Water,—reduce with Cold Water to 8° Twaddell. Rinse in this Liquor Five Minutes; Wring, and Rinse Five Minutes in Chrome Liquor, 3° Twaddell; put into Boiling Lime Water, and Rinse again Five Minutes.— Wash.

No. 97.

BLACK COLOUR.

5 Gallons Logwood Liquor, 12° Twaddell.
1   Do.   Red Liquor,   16°   do.
12 lbs. Flour.

Boil, and Cool to 110° Fahrenheit, add
2 Quarts Nitrate of Iron, 80° Twaddell.

No. 98.

DARK BLUE COLOUR.

5 Gallons Water.
7 ℔s. Starch.
6 ℔s. Gum Dragon.
  Boil,—cool to 160° Fahrenheit, and add
8 ℔s. Oxalic Acid.
1 Pint Vitriol.
6 ℔s. Prussiate of Potash.
6 ℔s. Sulphate of Iron.

Note.—When given out, add to 7 Measures of Colour 1 Measure Muriate of Tin.

No. 99.

LIGHT BLUE.

5 Quarts Dark Blue Standard.
1 Do. Gum Dragon.
1 Do. Double Muriate of Tin.

No. 100.

LIGHT PINK.

7 ℔s. Starch.
7 Gallons Sapanwood Liquor, 8° Twaddell.
           Boil, and then add
2 Gallons Gum Dragon, 140° Fahrenheit.
1½ ℔s. Salammonia.
18 Oz. Sulphate of Copper.
When giving out—to 16 Measures of the Colour,
           give
1 Measure Oxymuriate of Tin, 120° Twad.
           and
4   Do.   Double Muriate of Tin, 120° do.

No. 101.

DARK PINK.

3 Gallons Light Pink Colour, and add
½ Gill Nitrate of Copper.

No. 102.

DARK GREEN.

7 Quarts Gum Dragon.
1   Do.   Prussian Blue.
1   Do.   Nitric Acid to 12 of Colour.

No. 103.

LIGHT GREEN.

11 Quarts Gum Dragon.
1   Do.   Nitric Acid.
1   Do.   Prussian Blue.

No. 104.

PRUSSIAN BLUE FOR ORANGE GROUNDS.

3 lbs. Prussiate of Potash, dissolved in
1 Gallon Water, 212° Fahrenheit.
6 lbs. Nitrate of Copper, dissolved in
1 Gallon Water, 212° Fahrenheit.
Mix, by pouring the Nitrate on the Prussiate,
and add gradually,
2 Quarts of Nitric Acid.
Cool Twenty-four Hours.

Note.—These are all the Colours capable of being put on Orange Grounds.—To raise them, Rinse in Whitening Water, (4 lbs. Whitening to 20 Gallons Water,) for Ten Minutes, and then Wash well on Wheels.

No. 105.

YELLOW GROUNDS.

Same as No. 96, but the Chrome Liquor must be hot, and no Lime to be used.

SECTION VIII.

COLOURS FOR YELLOW GROUNDS.

No. 106.

PINK.

6 Gallons Sapanwood Liquor, 8° Twaddell.
6 ℔s. Starch.
Boil, and Cool to 110° Fahrenheit, then add
1 Measure Nitrate of Copper to
32   Do.   of Colour.
1   Do.   Oxymuriate of Tin, 12° Twad., to
8   Do.   of Colour.
            When giving out, take
4   Do.   of the above.
1   Do.   Double Muriate of Tin.

No. 107.

BLUE.

3 Measures Dark Orange Blue.
1   Do.   Gum Dragon.
12 of the above, and 1 of Double Muriate of Tin,
120° Twaddell.

No. 108.

GREEN STANDARD.

4 lbs. Brown Sugar of Lead.
        Dissolve and thicken with
1 ℔. Starch,— then dissolve
1 lb. Brown Chrome in
1 Gallon Gum Dragon Liquor.
        Mix well.

No. 109.

GREEN COLOUR.

8 Quarts Standard.
1   Do.   Prussian Blue.

No. 110.

WHITE FOR YELLOW OR ORANGE GROUNDS.

1 Gallon Gum Dragon Liquor.
1 Quart Double Muriate of Tin, 120° Twad.
Wash and Rinse same as No. 104.

SECTION IX.

SILK DYEING.

TO PREPARE CLOTH FOR SILK DYEING.

Bleach in a Copper pan or vessel capable of containing 100 Gallons of Water, in which dissolve 6 lbs. White Soap, 2 lbs. Soft Soap,—Boil, and turn on the Wince till perfectly white.

Note.—Madder Colours are dyed same as Cotton.

STEAM COLOURS FOR SILK.

No. 111.

BLUE STANDARD.

1 Gallon Water.
1½ lbs. Prussiate of Potash.
4 Oz. Tartaric Acid.

No. 112.

BLUE COLOUR.

1 Gallon Water, ⎫
2 Oz. Starch, ⎬ Boil, and add
1 Quart of Standard. ⎭
1 Do. Prussiate of Tin Pulp.

No. 113.

BLACK.

1 Gallon Logwood Liquor, 8° Twaddell.
1½ lbs. British Gum.
3 Oz. Common Salt.
3 Oz. Nitrate of Copper.
   Boil Fifteen Minutes, Cool, and add
3 Noggins Nitrate of Iron, 8° Twaddell.
1 Gill Muriate of Iron, 70° do.
1 Nitrate of Copper.

No. 114.

CHOCOLATE.

3 Pints Logwood Liquor, 8° Twaddell.
6 Do. Sapanwood do. 12° do.
2 Do. Bark do. 16° do.
2 ℔s. British Gum.

Boil, and add

2 Oz. Common Salt, at 110° Fahrenheit.
1 Gill Nitrate of Copper, 80° Twaddell.

No. 115.

DARK PURPLE.

3 Quarts Sapanwood Liquor, 8° Twaddell.
3 Noggins Red, do. 16° do.
1 lb. British Gum.

Boil, when Cold add

½ Gill Nitrate of Copper, 80° Twaddell.
4 Do. Archill Liquor.

No. 116.

ORANGE COLOUR.

1 Gallon Fustic Liquor, 8° Twaddell.
6 Gills Cochineal,   6°   do.
10 Oz. Starch.
   Boil,—Cool to 170° Fahrenheit, and add
3 Oz. Crystals of Tin, and at 110° Fah., add
8 Oz. Oxalic Acid.

No. 117.

GREEN COLOUR.

Same as No. 31,—other Colours similar to those
of Cotton.

No. 118.

TO DYE BLUE ON SILK.

Soak the Cloth, for One Hour, in Nitrate of
Iron, 60° Twaddell; Wash well; then raise in
Prussiate of Potash, at the rate of 1 oz ℔ Piece
of 7 yards.

No. 119.

WAX FOR SILK.

3 ℔s. Russian Tallow.
3½ ℔s. Unwrought Resin. } Melt together.

No. 120.

TO DYE PINK ON SILK.

Soak the Cloth, Two Hours, in Muriate, 20° Twaddell, then Wash. Put into the Copper for each piece of 7 yards,

10 Gallons Water.
  1 Oz. Bitartrate of Potash.
  2 Oz. Cochineal, Ground.

Bring to 160° Fahrenheit, and run the Cloth through it until the required Shade is got.

SECTION X.

MOUSSELINE D'LAINE PRINTING.

No. 121.

TO PREPARE THE CLOTH.

Soak or run the Cloth through Stannate of Potash Liquor, 8° Twad.,—Wash and Dry,—again Soak for 1½ Hours in Sulpho-Muriate of Tin, 8° Twad.,—then take goods out and drain them for Half an Hour, after which rinse them 10 Minutes in a Composition of Chloride of Lime and Vitriol, —take out and Wash for 15 Minutes,—Dry and pass the Cloth through a hot Calender, allowing it to Cool before Printing.

No. 122.

SULPHO-MURIATE OF TIN.

4 Gallons Water.—Dissolve
16 lbs. Murate of Tin Crystals. Add, by degrees,
32 lbs. Vitriol.

Mix well and reduce to 8° Twaddell.

No. 123.

CHLORIDE OF LIME STANDARD.

60 Gallons Water.   Add
 8   Do.   Fresh Chloride of Lime Liquor, 8° T.
 1 Quart Vitriol.
Mix well, and run off after every 20 Pieces.

No. 124.

LIGHT BLUE FOR TWO BLUES.

1 Quart of Standard, No. 126.
4   Do.   Gum Water.

No. 125.

ROYAL DARK BLUE.

 4 Gallons Water.
 8 lbs. Starch.   Boil well, and add
10 lbs. Tartaric Acid. }
12 Oz. Oxalic Acid.   } Dissolve, and add
 2 Gallons Prussiate of Tin Pulp.
    Mix well, and Strain for use.

No. 126.

PALE ROYAL BLUE STANDARD.

4 Gallons Water. ⎫
6 lbs. Starch. ⎬ Boil well, and add
6 lbs. Tartaric Acid, dissolve.
15 Oz. Oxalic Acid.
2 Gallons Prussiate of Tin Pulp.
6 lbs. Prussiate of Potash.
    Strain well,—it is then ready for use.

No. 127.

DARK SCARLET.

2 Gallons Cochineal Liquor, 7° Twaddell.
2 lbs. Starch.   Boil well, and add
1 Quart of Bark Liquor.
8 Oz. Tin Crystals,—when at 110° Fah., add
8 Oz. Oxalic Acid.
    Dissolve, and Strain for use.

No. 128.

PALE RED STANDARD.

2 Quarts Ammonia,   ⎱ soak 24 Hours, and
4 ℔s. Silver Cochineal, ⎰   add
2 Gallons Water, 212° Fahrenheit.

Boil well for One Hour; Strain off the Liquor, and add other 2 Gallons Water; Boil another Hour, and then Strain through a Hair Sieve, observing that the Liquor has boiled down to 2 Gallons.

No. 129.

PALE RED COLOUR.

1 Gallon Standard.   Dissolve in it
8 Oz. Alum.
6 Oz. Bitartrate of Potash, and
3 Gallons Gum Senegal Liquor.

No. 130.

CRIMSON COLOUR.

1 Gallon Pale Red Standard, thickened with
4 ℔s. Gum Senegal.

No. 131.

LIGHT RED BLOTCH CHOCOLATE.

4 Gallons Sapanwood Liquor, 12° Twaddell.
1 Do. Logwood do. 12° do.
5 ℔s. British Gum,
5 ℔s. Gum Substitute,—Boil well, and add
1¼ ℔s. Salammonia.
3¼ ℔s. Alum.
2½ ℔s. Red Prussiate of Potash.
1 Gallon Bark Liquor.
9 Oz. Chloride of Potash.
    Mix well, and Strain for use.

No. 132.

DARK CHOCOLATE FOR BLEACHING.

3 Gallons Sapanwood Liquor, 8° Twaddell.
2 Do. Logwood do. 12° do.
5 ℔s. British Gum.
3 ℔s. Gum Substitute,—Boil, and add
3 ℔s. 2 oz. Alum.
3 ℔s. 2 oz. Red Prussiate of Potash, and
5 Oz. Chloride of Potash.

No. 133.

DARK PRINTING CHOCOLATE.

2 Gallons Sapanwood Liquor, 12° Twaddell.
1 Do. Logwood   do. 12°   do.
3 ℔s. Starch,—Boil well, and add
3 ℔s. Red Prussiate of Potash.
3 ℔s. Alum.
4 Oz. Chloride of Potash,
1 Oz. Brown Chrome.
        Mix well, and Strain for use.

No. 134.

SINGLE GREEN.

1½ ℔s. Starch.
1 Gallon Berry Liquor, 4° Twaddell.
8 Oz. Alum.
1 Gill Vinegar.
3 Oz. Muriate of Tin, 120° Twaddell.
12 Oz. Prussiate of Potash.
1 Oz. Oxalic Acid.

Note.—28 Measures of the above to 1 of Extract of Indigo, forms the Colour.

No. 135.

PALE GREEN STANDARD.

Same as 134, but Berry Liquor to be only 3° Twaddell.

No. 136.

DARK GREEN.

3 Quarts Bark Liquor, 18° Twaddell.
1 Do. Berry do. 12° do.
1 ℔. Gum Substitute,—Boil, and add
12 Oz. Alum.
7 Oz. Muriate of Tin, 120° Twaddell.
8 Oz. Tartaric Acid.
4 Oz. Oxalic Acid.
1 Gill Vinegar.
1 Noggin Prussiate of Tin Pulp.
1 Pint Extract of Indigo.
     Mix well, and Strain for use.

No. 137.

BLACK COLOUR.

4½ lbs. Flour.
1 lb. British Gum, } Dissolved in
3 Gallons Logwood Liquor, 8° Twaddell.
1 lb. Salammonia.
Boil, and Cool to 110° Fahrenheit; then add
1 Pint Vinegar.
3 Noggins Muriate of Iron, 70° Twaddell.
3 Do. Nitrate of Iron, 80° do.
3 Gills Extract of Indigo.
¾ Noggin of Nitrate of Copper, 80° T.

No. 138.

DOVE STANDARD.

FIRST SHADE.

1 Gallon 4 lb.-Lavender, No. 139.
2 Quarts 1½ lb.-Prussiate Liquor, No. 140.
1 lb. Extract of Indigo.
Thicken full Strength.

SECOND SHADE.

1 Measure of No. 138.
2   Do. Gum Senegal Liquor.

THIRD SHADE.

1 Measure of No. 138.
5   Do. Gum Senegal Liquor.

No. 139.

4℔.-LAVENDER.

4 ℔s. Ground Logwood, soaked 48 Hours in
1 Gallon Red Liquor, 16° Twad., 140° Fah.

No. 140.

1½℔.-PRUSSIATE LIQUOR.

1½ ℔s. Prussiate of Potash, dissolved in
1 Gallon Water.

No. 141.

DRAB.

4 Measures Single Purple.
4   Do.   No. 2-Peg Blue.
1   Do.   Strong Yellow.

No. 142.

STRONG YELLOW.

1 Gallon Persian Berry Liquor, 12° Twaddell,
         thicken with
3 ℔s. Gum Senegal,—Boil, and add
12 Oz. Alum.
      Dissolve, and Strain for use.

No. 143.

No. 2-PEG BLUE.

1 Measure Common Blue Standard, No. 40.
2   Do   Gum Senegal.

No. 144.

STONE STANDARD.

2 Quarts of Lavender.
3 Do. 16-Blue Standard.
1 Strong Yellow.

No. 145.

STONE COLOUR.

3 Measures Gum Water.
1 Do. Stone Standard.

No. 146.

FRENCH WHITE STANDARD.

12 Measures 4℔.-Lavender.
4 Do. Strong Yellow.
1 Do. 16-Blue Standard.

No. 147.

FRENCH WHITE COLOUR.

8 Measures Gum Water.
1   Do.   French White Standard.

No. 148.

16-BLUE STANDARD.

$1\frac{1}{2}$ fbs. Prussiate of Potash.
3   Quarts Cold Water.
8   Oz. Tartaric Acid.
2   Oz. Vitriol.
2   Oz. Oxalic Acid.
            Dissolve.

No. 149.

BLUE COLOUR.

1 Measure of 16-Blue Standard.
1   Do.   Gum Water.

Note.—16 Measures of the above to 1 of Extract of Indigo.

No. 150.

OLIVE DRAB STANDARD.

3 Measures of 4lb.-Lavender.
2   Do.   16-Blue.
1   Do.   Strong Yellow.
1½   Do.   Fawn Standard.

No. 151.

OLIVE DRAB COLOUR.

1 Measure Standard.
4   Do.   Gum Senegal Water.

No. 152.

FAWN STANDARD.

6 Measures of Yellow.
4   Do.   Lavender.
1   Do.   Dark Royal Purple.

No. 153.

FAWN COLOUR.

48 Measures of Standard. ⎫
1   Do.   16-Blue. ⎬ Mix well.
                          ⎭

No. 154.

DARK ROYAL PURPLE.

1 Gallon Logwood Liquor, 5° Twaddell.
4 ℔s. Gum Substitute.
1 ℔. Alum.
8 Oz. Red Prussiate of Potash,
1 Oz. Oxalic Acid.
1 Oz. Super-Oxilate of Potash.

No. 155.

SLATE STANDARD.

5 Measures of 16-Blue.
4   Do.   Lavender.

No. 156.

SLATE COLOUR.

1 Measure Standard.
4   Do   Gum Water.

No. 157.

DARK COPPER BROWN STANDARD.

2 Quarts of Bark Liquor, 12° Twaddell.
2   Do.   Berry do. 12°   do.
2   Do.   Red   do. 16°   do.
1½ Do.   Logwood do. 12°   do.
3   Do.   Sapanwood do. 8°   do.
            Dissolve in it
8 lbs. Senegal Gum.
8 Oz. Salammonia.
8 Oz. Alum.
8 Oz. Sulphate of Copper.
      At 110° Fahrenheit, add
1 Quart Nitrate of Copper, 80° Twaddell.

No. 158.

CHROME BROWN STANDARD.

2 Gallons of Bark Liquor, . . . 12° Twad.
1½   Do.   Sapanwood Liquor, 12°   do.
1 Quart of Red   do.   16°   do.
1   Do.   Logwood   do.   12°   do.
8 Oz. Alum ℔ Gallon.
4 Oz. Red Prussiate of Potash.
¼ Oz. Brown Chrome ℔ Gallon.
    Thicken with Gum Substitute.

No. 159.

DARK BROWN FOR TWO COLOURS.

4 Measures of Strong Yellow.
2   Do.   Dark Blotch Chocolate.
1   Do.   Lavender.

No. 160.

DARK BROWN FOR RAINBOWING.

3 Measures of Strong Yellow.
1   Do.   Chrome Brown Standard.
1   Do.   Lavender, and
1   Do.   Printing Chocolate, to
8   Do.   Dark Brown Colour.

No. 161.

SINGLE BROWN STANDARD.

3 Measures of Strong Yellow.
1   Do.   Chrome Brown.
1   Do.   Lavender.

No. 162.

SINGLE BROWN COLOUR.

8 Measures of Standard.
1   Do.   Lavender.

No. 163.

VERY DARK BROWN.

6 Measures of Dark Brown Chrome.
1   Do.   Strong Yellow.
1   Do.   Blotch Chocolate.

No. 164.

PALE BROWN FOR TWO BROWNS.

1 Measure of Single Brown.
2   Do.   Gum Water.

No. 165.

FRENCH BROWN STANDARD.

1 Measure of Crimson.
1   Do.   Lavender.
1   Do.   Strong Yellow.—Mix well.

No. 166.

FRENCH BROWN COLOUR.

1 Measure of Standard.
3   Do.   Gum Water.

No. 167.

OLIVE BROWN STANDARD.

12 Measures of Strong Yellow.
 3   Do.   Chrome Brown.
 2   Do.   Blotch Chocolate.

No. 168.

RESIST STONE STANDARD.

2 Measures of Dark Crimson for Dahlias.
1½   Do.   4℔.-Lavender Liquor.
1   Do.   Logwood Liquor, 8° Twaddell.
1½   Do.   Strong Yellow.
2   Do.   Neutral Sulphate of Indigo.

No. 169.

RESIST STONE COLOUR.

9 ℔s. Spanish Whitening.
1 Quart of Standard.
1 Do.   Water.
Beat up to the consistency of thick Paste,—add
5 Quarts of Barbary Gum.
Mix well, and Strain for use.

No. 170.

SULPHATE OF INDIGO.

1 ℔. of Best Spanish Indigo Ground,—Mix in
4 Quarts of Double Vitriol.
Let stand in a hot place Forty-eight Hours;
stir occasionally with a Glass Rod; to neutralize
it, add, by degrees, 1 ℔. of Spanish Whitening
to the above quantity. Observe that all the
Free Acid is off, which will not be till Effervescence ceases.

SECTION XI.

STANDARDS FOR THE VARIOUS SHADES

OF

STONES, DRABS, BUFFS, OLIVES, & BROWNS.

No. 171.

A. STANDARD.

2 Gallons of Water,—Dissolve in it,

12 lbs. Good Catechu.

12 Oz. Salammonia.

1 Gallon of Gum Water.

3 Pints Nitrate of Copper. 80° Twaddell.

No. 171.

B. STANDARD.

2 Gallons of Water.

7 lbs. Catechu.

12 Oz. Salammonia.

1 Gallon of Gum Water.

3 Pints Nitrate of Copper, 80° Twaddell.

No. 172.

BLUE LIQUOR.

1 Gallon Water.
8 Oz. Tartaric Acid.
8 Oz. Alum.
1 Pint Extract of Indigo.

No. 1 Dark Shade.

5 Measures of A. Standard.
2   Do.   Fustic, 8° Twaddell.
2   Do.   Lavender.

No. 2 Light Shade.

3 Measures of B. Standard.
2   Do.   Fustic, 8° Twaddell.
1   Do.   Lavender.
11   Do.   Gum.
            Mix well.

No. 3 Shade, Standard.

1 Measure of B. Standard.
1   Do.   Fustic, 8° Twaddell.
12 Do.   Lavender.

No. 4 Shade, Colour.

1 Measure Standard.
16 Do. Gum.
¼ Do. Blue Liquor.

No. 4 Shade, Standard.

4 Measures of Royal Purple.
3   Do.   B. Standard.
1   Do.   - Blue Liquor.

No. 4 Shade, Colour.

1 Measure, No. 4, Standard.
1   Do. Gum.
1   Do. Blue Liquor.

No. 173.

DARK PURPLE FOR DAHLIAS.

1 Gallon of Fresh Boiled Logwood Liquor, 5° Twaddell.
2 lbs. Senegal Gum.
1 lb. Alum.
8 Oz. Red Prussiate of Potash.
1 Oz. Oxalic Acid.
1 Oz. Super-Oxalate of Potash.

No. 174.

CRIMSON STANDARD FOR DAHLIAS.

1 Gallon Ammonia,—Steep
2 lbs. Cochineal, Forty-eight Hours.
Boil in One Gallon Water, Two Hours; keep up to One Gallon; strain off your Liquor, and add
3 Oz. Cream of Tartar.
3 Oz. Oxalic Acid.
8 Oz. Alum, —thicken with
2 lbs. Senegal Gum.

No. 175.

DARK DAHLIA.

1 Quart Crimson.
1 Do. Dark Royal Purple.
$\frac{1}{8}$ Do. Blue Liquor.

SECOND SHADE.

1 Measure of Dark Royal Purple.
2 Do. Crimson.
6 Do. Gum Water.

THIRD SHADE.

1 Measure of Dark Royal Purple.
3 Do. Crimson.
18 Do. Gum Water.

No. 176.

PURPLE SHADE.

2 Measures of Dark Royal Purple.
1 Do. Single Purple.

SECOND SHADE.

1 Measure of Dark Royal Purple.
2   Do.   Gum Water.

THIRD SHADE.

1 Measure of Dark Royal Purple.
2   Do.   Lavender.
12   Do.   Gum Water.

No. 177.

SINGLE PURPLE.

1 Gallon 4 ℔.-Lavender.
3 ℔s. Senegal Gum.
3 Oz. Super-Oxalate of Potash.

Note.—To every 80 Measures add 1 Measure of No. 16-Blue.

No. 178.

CLARET.

3 Quarts of Sapanwood Liquor, 8° Twaddell.
1 Do. Logwood Liquor, 8° do.
2 ℔s. Senegal Gum.
12 Ox. Alum.
8 Oz. Salammonia.
Boil, and Cool to 100° Fahrenheit; then add
1 Glass Nitrate of Copper, 80° Twaddell.

No. 179.

BUFF STANDARD.

2 ℔s. of Best French Madder.
1 Gallon Red Liquor, 16° Twad., 160° Fahr.
Steep Six Hours, then Strain off the Liquor.

No. 180.

BUFF COLOUR.

1 Measure of Standard.
½ Do. Berry Liquor, 12° Twaddell.
3 Do. Gum Water.

No. 181.

EXTRACT OF INDIGO.

1 ℔. Best Fine Ground Indigo.
6 ℔s. Double Vitriol.
Mix together; let stand Forty-eight Hours in a Stone Pot, then put the Vessel into a Warm Bath till properly dissolved; take
6 Gallons Water, 170° Fahrenheit.
Add the Indigo slowly, then Filter through Woollen Cloth, covered with Brown Paper, into a Wooden Vessel; what remains on the Paper put away, as it is only earth, then add to your Liquor
4 ℔s. Common Salt.
1 ℔. Pearl Ash.

Note.—Let stand till it ceases Fermenting, then Filter again through Brown Paper, and what remains on the Paper is Pure Extract of Indigo. There should be 12 ℔s. of it.

No. 182.

EXTRACT OF COPPER.

1 Gallon Extract of Indigo.
1   Do.   Nitrate of Copper, 80° Twaddell.
Mix together; set in a warm place till Effervescence ceases.

No. 183.

RESIST GOLD.

1 Gallon Persian Berry Liquor, 12° Twaddell.
1 ℔. Starch.

    Boil well, and add

4 Oz. Tin Crystals.
2 lbs. Sulphate of Zinc.
2 Oz. Oxalic Acid.

    Dissolve, and Strain for use.

No. 184.

BERRY YELLOW.

1 Gallon Berry Liquor, 3° Twaddell.
3 ℔s. Gum Substitute,—Boil, and add
8 Oz. Alum.

No. 185.

ORANGE.

11 Quarts Persian Berry Liquor, 12° Twad.
  Do. Cochineal,   6° do.
2½ ℔s. Starch,—Boil, and add
12 Oz. Tin Crystals.
 9 Oz. Oxalic Acid, 110° Fahrenheit.

No. 186.

YELLOW.

Same Ingredients as Orange, omitting the Cochineal.

No. 187.

STANDARDS FOR SHADES OF CATECHU.

A. STANDARD.

$2\frac{1}{2}$ ℔s. Catechu.
1 Gallon Water.
4 Oz. Salammonia.
1 Pint Nitrate of Copper.

———

B. STANDARD.

2 Quarts of Bark Liquor, 12° Twaddell.
2 Do. Berry Liquor, 12° do.
8 Oz. Alum.

———

C. STANDARD.

1 Gallon Lavender.
3 Oz. Super-Oxalate of Potash.
1 Gill Logwood Liquor, 8° Twaddell.

D. STANDARD.

1 Gallon Water.
4 Oz. Tartaric Acid.
8 Oz. Alum.
2 ℔s. Extract.

———

FIRST SHADE.

1 Measure of A. Standard.
1   Do.   B. Standard.
1   Do.   D. Standard.
3   Do.   Gum Water.

———

SECOND SHADE.

2 Measures of A. Standard.
$\frac{1}{2}$ Do.   C. Standard.
$2\frac{1}{2}$ Do.   B. Standard.
8   Do.   Gum Water.

THIRD SHADE.

2 Measures of D. Standard.
$\frac{1}{4}$ Do. A. Standard.
3 Do. B. Standard.
12 Do. Gum Water.

FOURTH SHADE.

6 Measures of A. Standard.
1 Do. C. Standard.
$\frac{1}{2}$ Do. D. Standard.
8 Do. Gum Water.

SECTION XII.

MISCELLANEOUS RECEIPTS.

No. 188.

PREPARATIONS FOR WOOLLEN GOODS.

Steep in Sulpho-Muriate of Tin, at 10° Twad-dell, Two Hours,—drain One Hour, then run through Chrome Liquor, at $\frac{1}{4}$° Twaddell. Wash and dry in an Air Shade.

No. 189.

SULPHO-MURIATE OF TIN FOR WOOLS.

$1\frac{1}{2}$ lbs. Vitriol.
1 lb. Tin Crystals.
          Dissolve in Cold Water.

No. 190.

NITRO-MURIATE OF TIN.

10 ℔s. Nitric Acid.—Add to it slowly,
6 ℔s. Muriate of Tin Crystals.
Let Stand all Night before using.

No. 191.

HOW TO MAKE ACETIC ACID.

60   ℔s. White Sugar of Lead,—Dissolve in
7½ Gallons of Water.
When at 110° Fahrenheit, add
4½ Quarts Oil of Vitriol.
Use the Clear Liquor.

No. 192.

PASTE FOR RESISTING FAST BUFF.

3 Quarts Citrate of Soda, Thickened with Pipeclay.
3 Quarts Gum Water.

No. 193.

CITRATE OF SODA.

3 Quarts Custic Soda, 70° Twaddell.
5   Do. Lime Juice, 50°   do.
Mix well, and let Stand till Fermentation ceases.

No. 194.

ANNATO ORANGE STANDARD.

4 ℔s. Good Annato,—Dissolve in
1 Gallon Caustic Potash Liquor, at 16° Twad.,
              Strain and add
3 Oz. Alum.
1 Gill Red Liquor, 16° Twaddell.

No. 195.

ANNATO ORANGE COLOUR.

1 Measure Standard.
1   Do.   Yellow.
3   Do.   Gum Water.
            Mix.

No. 196.

ANNATO YELLOW.

1 Gallon Berry Liquor, 3° Twaddell.
8 Oz. Alum.

Boil.

FRENCH ORANGES.—MORDANTS.

No. 197.

DARK MORDANT.

4 lbs. Brown Sugar of Lead, ⎫
2 lbs. Nitrate of Lead, ⎬ Dissolve in
1 Gallon of Water,—Thicken with ⎭
2 lbs. British Gum.

Boil and Strain.

No. 198.

PALE STANDARD.

10 Oz. Brown Sugar of Lead,—Dissolve in
 1 Gallon of Water,—Thicken with
 1½ ℔s. British Gum.

No. 199.

TO RAISE MORDANTS.

Run through Sulphate of Soda Liquor, at 17°
Twaddell, 180° Fahrenheit, one Piece per Mi-
nute,—Wash 10 Minutes, then Turn 10 times in
Chrome Copper separately,—add 5 Quarts Caus-
tic Potash Lye, 27° Twaddell to the Chrome,—
turn 20 times in that,—take out and Rinse in
Clean Water,—then give 6 turns in Weak Lime
Water,—Wash and Finish.

No. 200.

SULPHATE OF SODA.

60 ℔s. Glauber Salts,—Dissolve in Water; and add,

5 ℔s. Vitriol, slowly.

Reduce to 17° Twaddell.

No. 201.

CHROME COPPER.

2½ ℔s. Brown Chrome.

50 Gallons Water.

Make up with Strong Chrome Liquor at the end of every 10 Pieces.

No. 202.

RESIST PASTE FOR COVERING WITH BLUE.

3½ ℔s. Sulphate of Zinc.

Dissolve in 2 Quarts of Water,—Thicken with Pipeclay,—then Melt, in 2 Quarts Gum Water, 8 Oz. Soft Soap, and Mix it with the above,—then Strain for use.

No. 202.

PASTE FOR GREEN.

6 lbs. Epsom Salts.

Dissolve in 2 Quarts of Water,—Thicken with Pipeclay,—then Melt, in 2 Quarts Gum Water, 12 Oz. Soft Soap, and Mix with the above,— then Strain for use.

FINIS.